color with purpose

AN UNCONVENTIONAL COLORING BOOK FOR REMARKABLE HUMANS

Megan Atkinson

ISBN-13: 978-1539965558
ISBN-10: 1539965554

You have not
come this far

to only
come this far

HOW TO USE THIS BOOK

Dearest remarkable human,

I am not much a fan of rules so I won't impose any on you here. But I do want to explain the purpose of this coloring book (and then some) as well as my hopes and dreams for its impact on you.

This coloring book was not created for the purpose of relaxation, meditation, or quiet time-wasting. It was created in hopes that remarkable humans such as yourself would be inspired to dig deep, reflect on the possibilities that lie ahead, and feel a little fire under your rump to make the most of your days.

This book contains six primary themes, or chapters if you will. Each chapter represents a piece of what I feel makes remarkable people super special. Each chapter contains a visual manifesto, three coloring pages featuring inspirational quotes, and three writing prompts to help you reflect, ponder, and celebrate what makes you remarkable.

Start at the front and work your way to the end... or pick a page that inspires the pants off ya - that's totally up to you. But please, pretty please, use this book to inspire an extra dose of awesome in your day-to-day life.

Peace, love, and colored pencils,

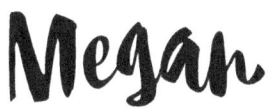

FOR THE DOER

carpe that damn diem.
wake up. kick ass. repeat.
keep showing up.
don't wait for permission.
finish what you start.
do the thing
that freakin' terrifies you.
hustle like there's
no tomorrow.
say no to mediocrity.

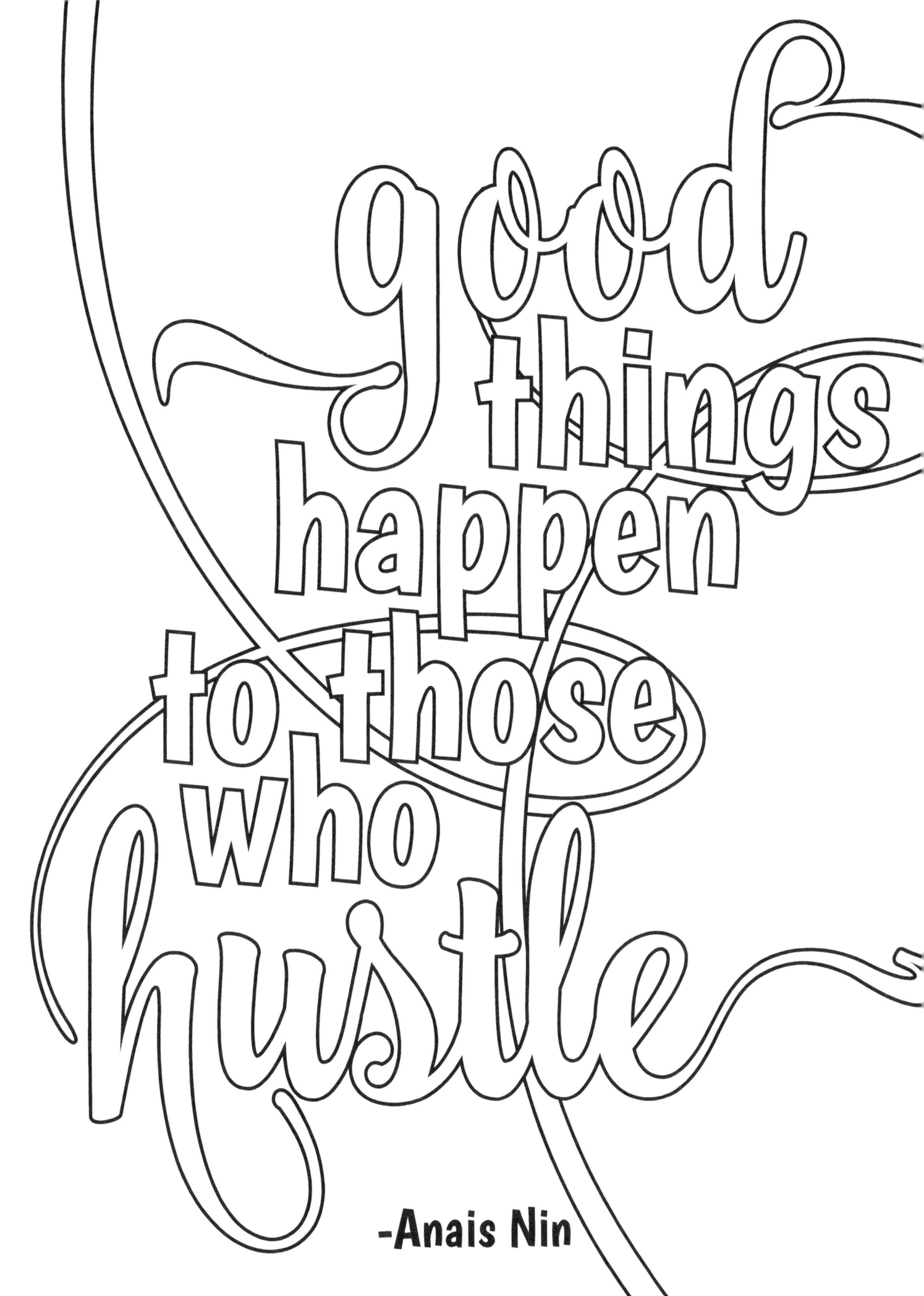

good things happen to those who hustle

-Anais Nin

Describe the last time you did something for the first time.

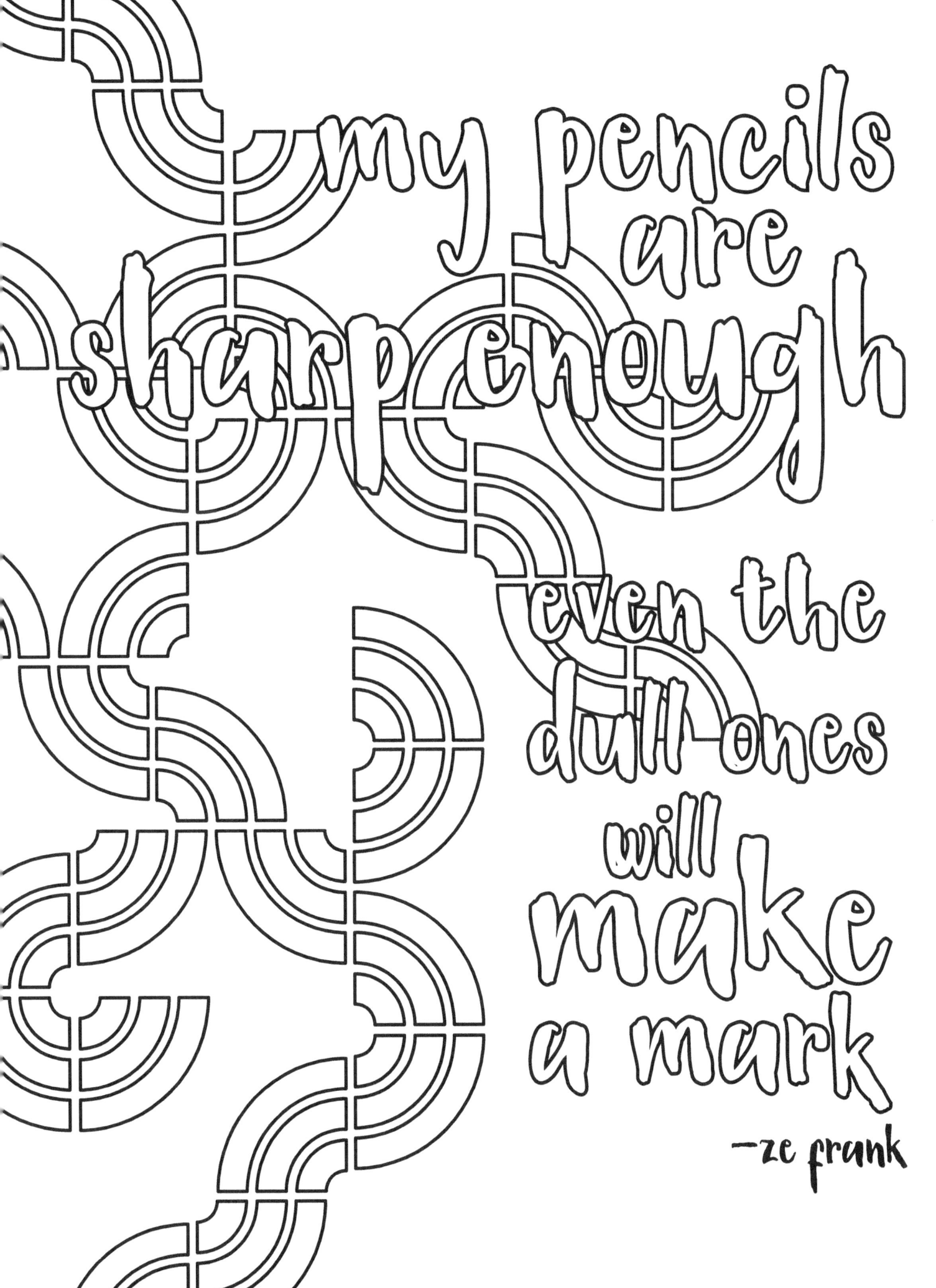

What have you been dying to do but haven't started yet?

I WILL STRAIN MY POTENTIAL UNTIL IT CRIES FOR MERCY

-Og Mandino

What do you aspire to be fearless at?

hustle

FOR THE DREAMER

want it more than you fear it.
the world needs your
brand of magic.
be unstoppable.
redefine what's possible.
do what they say you cannot do.
believe in
your wildest dreams.
don't let your dreams become
the goals of yesteryear.
let your dreams
shout louder than your fears.

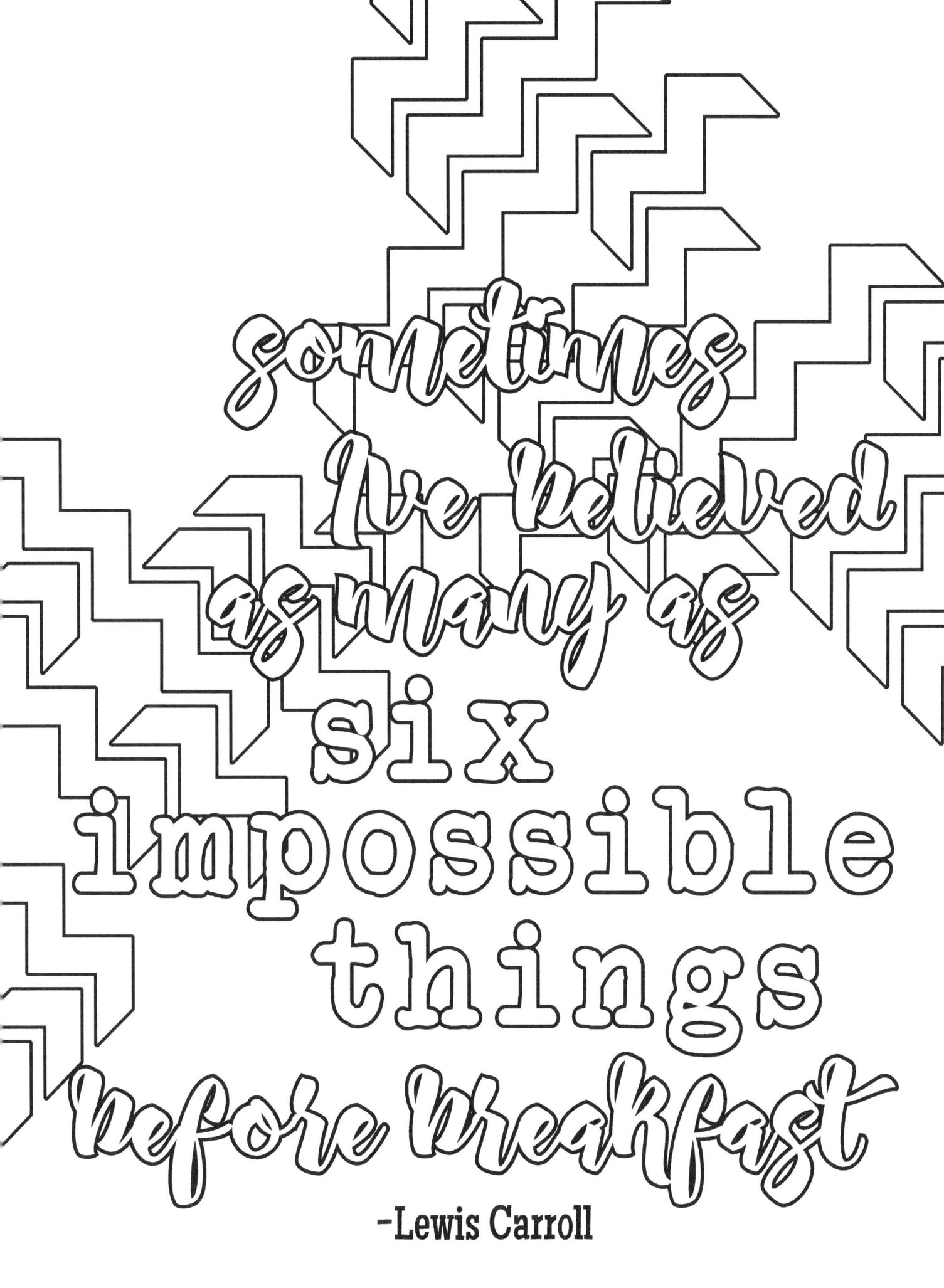

Sometimes I've believed as many as six impossible things before breakfast

-Lewis Carroll

What have you achieved that you once felt was impossible?

you musn't be afraid to Dream a little Bigger darling

-Christopher Nolan

Beyond your goals, beyond your big ideas, what is your heart's desire? What are your wildest dreams?

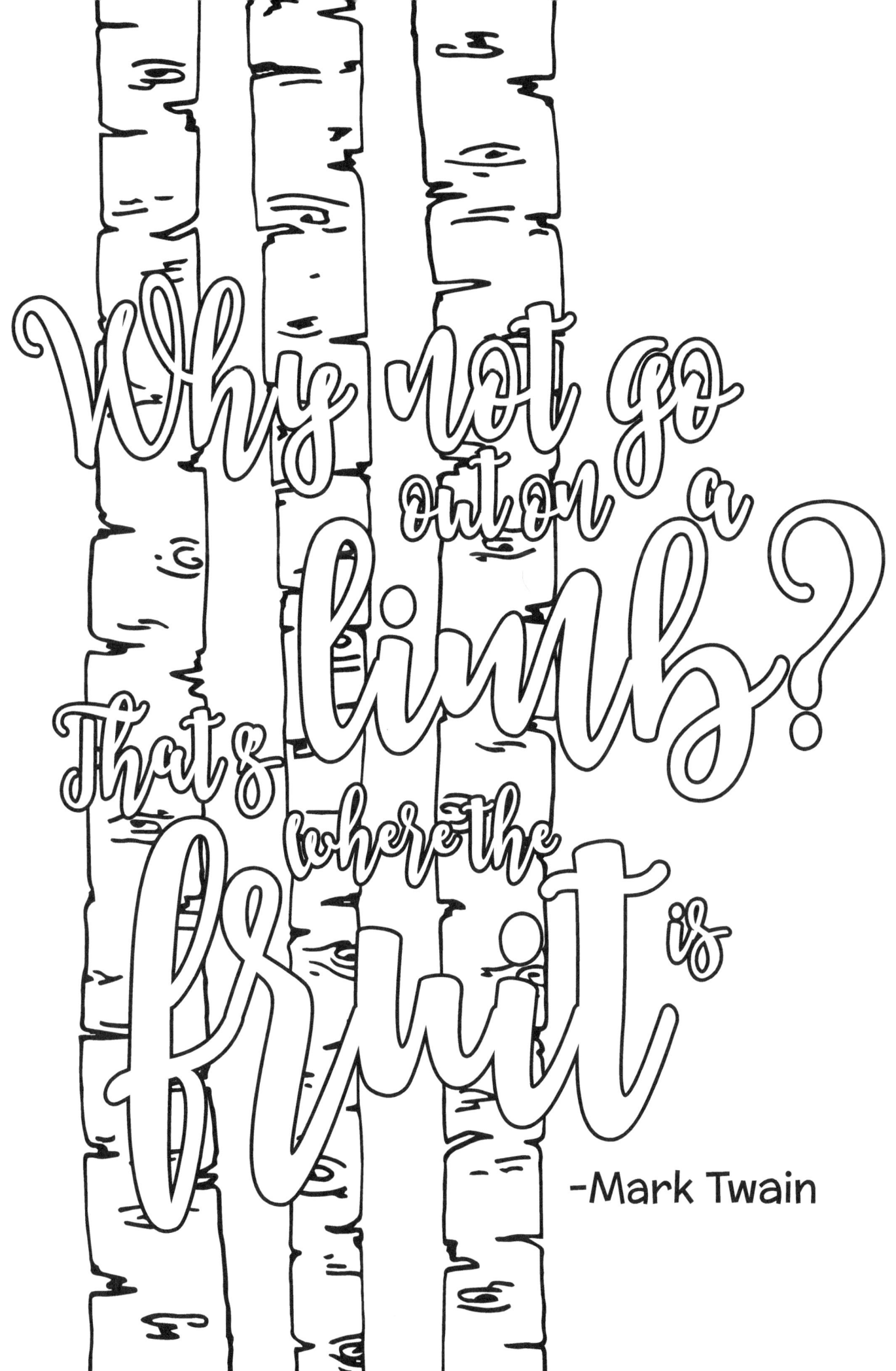

Why not go out on a limb? That's where the fruit is

-Mark Twain

When have you made the hard decision to chase what you want rather than listen to what you fear?

imagine

FOR THE CREATIVE

share your truth
with the world.
make something beautiful.
fix what's broken and
reinvent what's not.
experiment
every damn day.
use your voice.
don't keep your talents a secret.
tell your story.
embrace the messy bits.

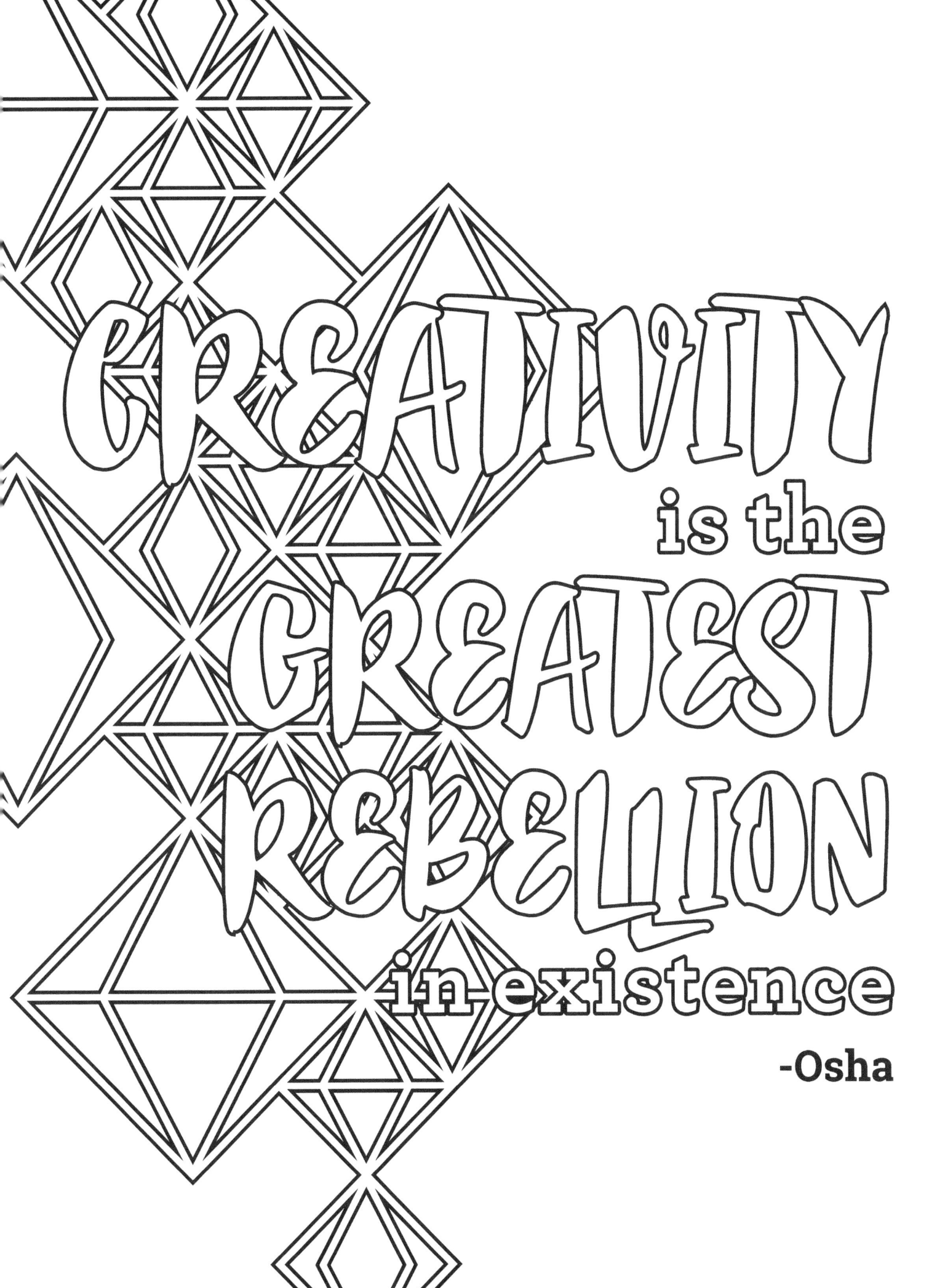

CREATIVITY is the GREATEST REBELLION in existence

-Osha

What would you like to learn to create with your own two hands?

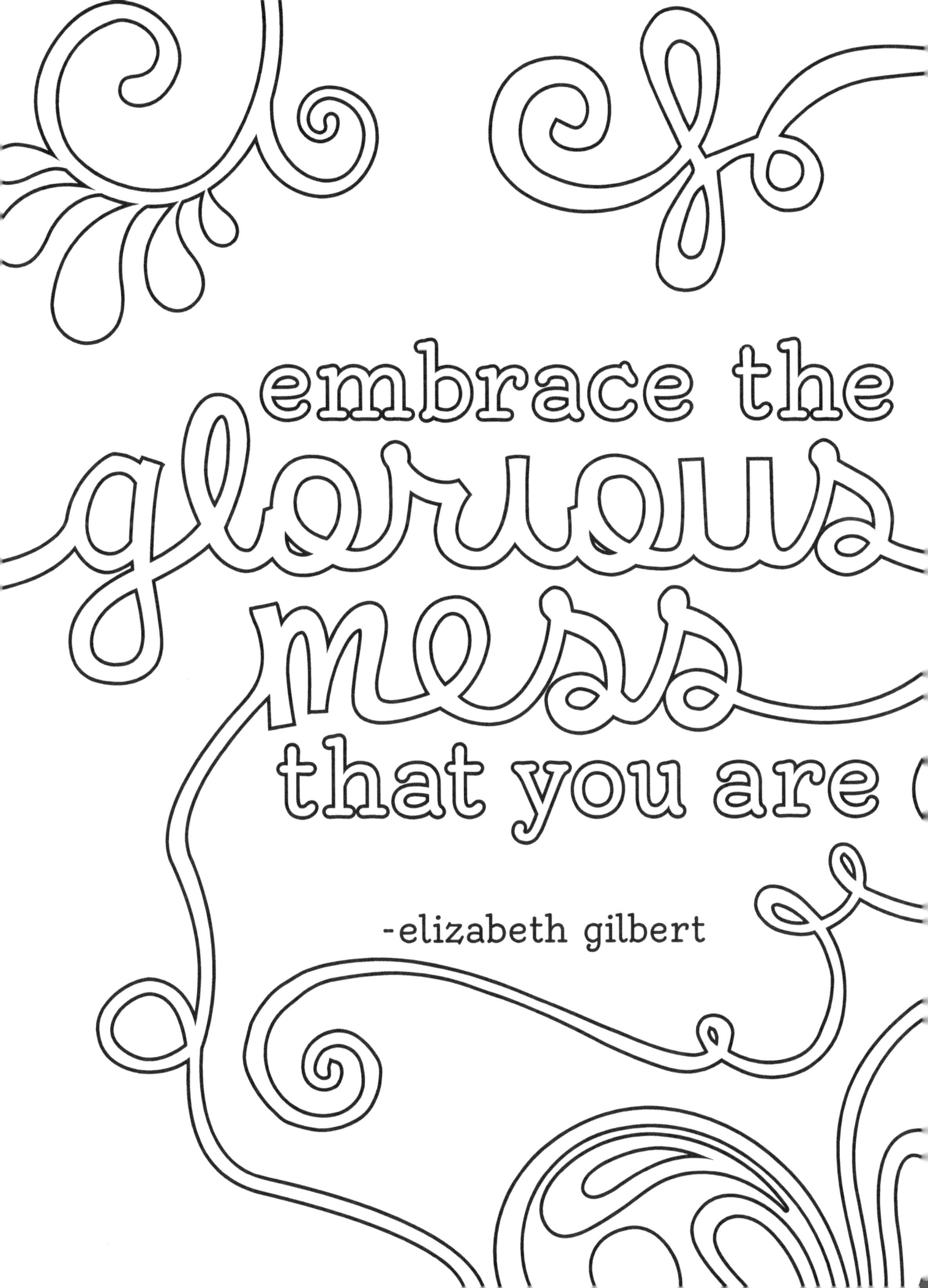

Which creative quirks (that others just don't understand) are you no longer willing to apologize for?

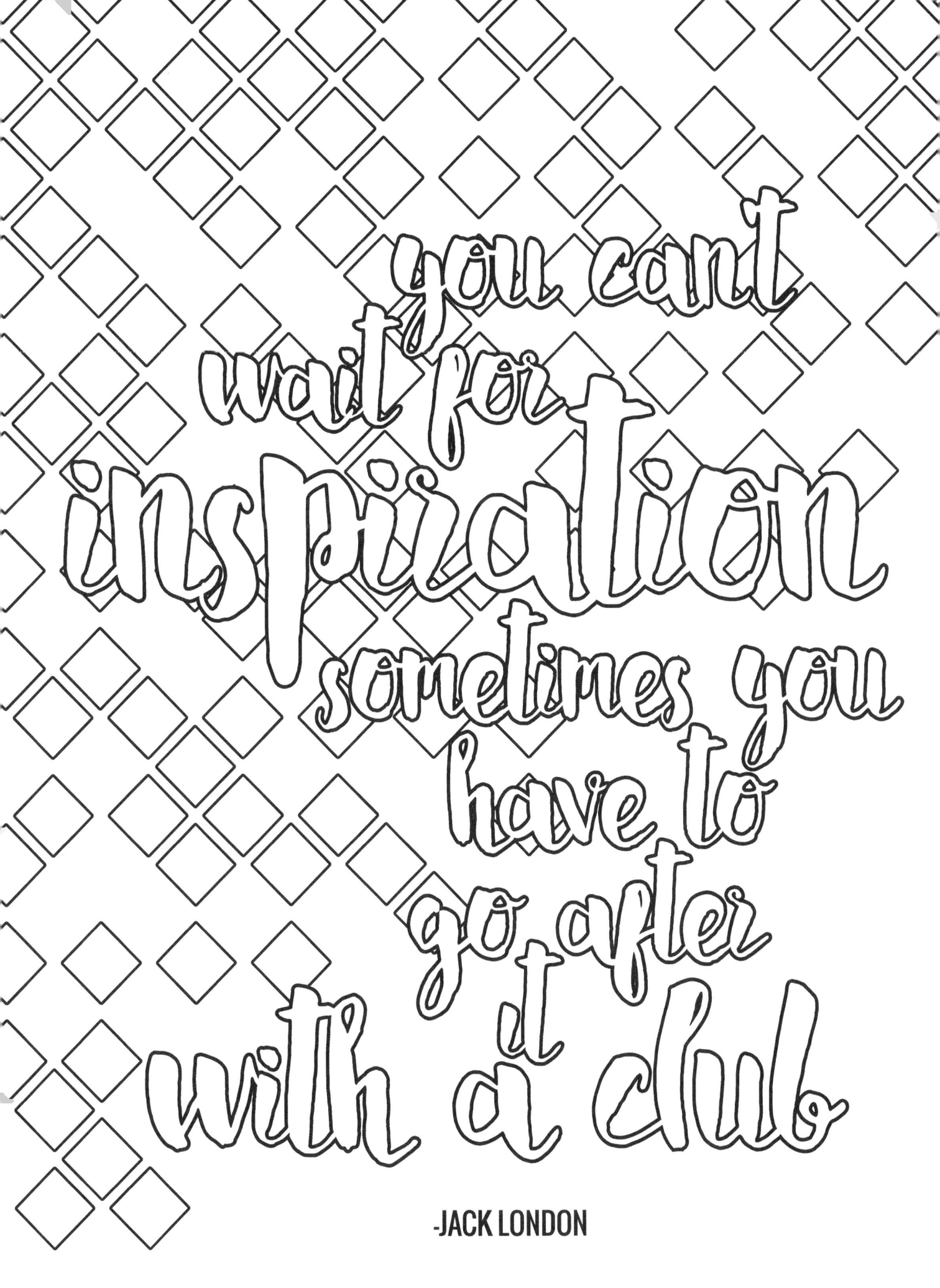

you cant wait for inspiration sometimes you have to go after it with a club

-JACK LONDON

What can you create today so you can be ready when inspiration strikes?

make

FOR THE EXPLORER

take time to wander.
never stop exploring.
enjoy every minute
of the journey.
go someplace you've
never gone before.
be an everyday adventurer.
take the scenic route.
get lost.
embrace the detours.

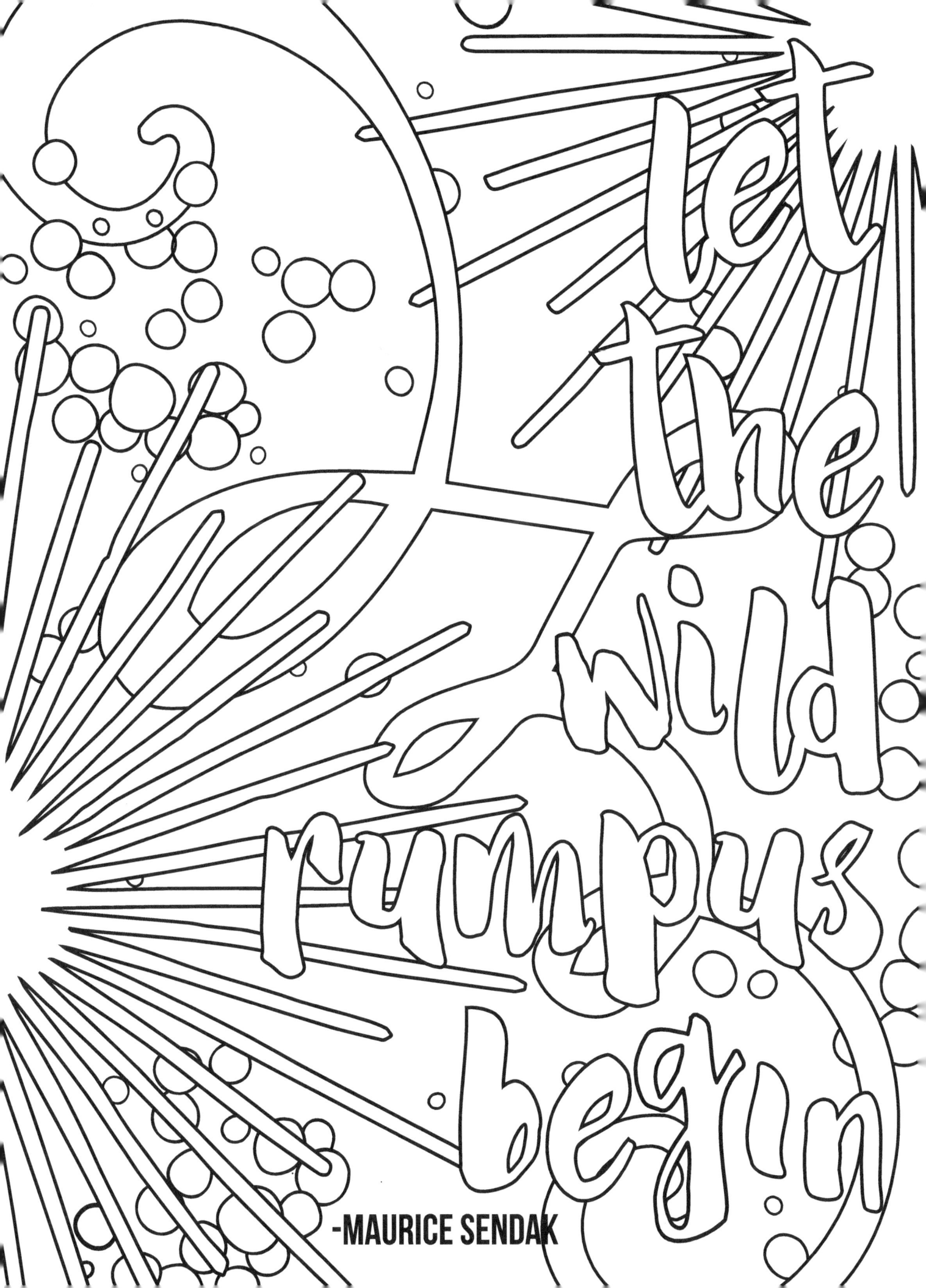

let the wild rumpus begin

-MAURICE SENDAK

List the adventures you're dying to take and explorations you're aching to make.

NOT ALL THOSE WHO WANDER ARE LOST

-J.R.R. TOLKIEN

What amazing things could come your way if you were to ditch "the plan" and move on without one?

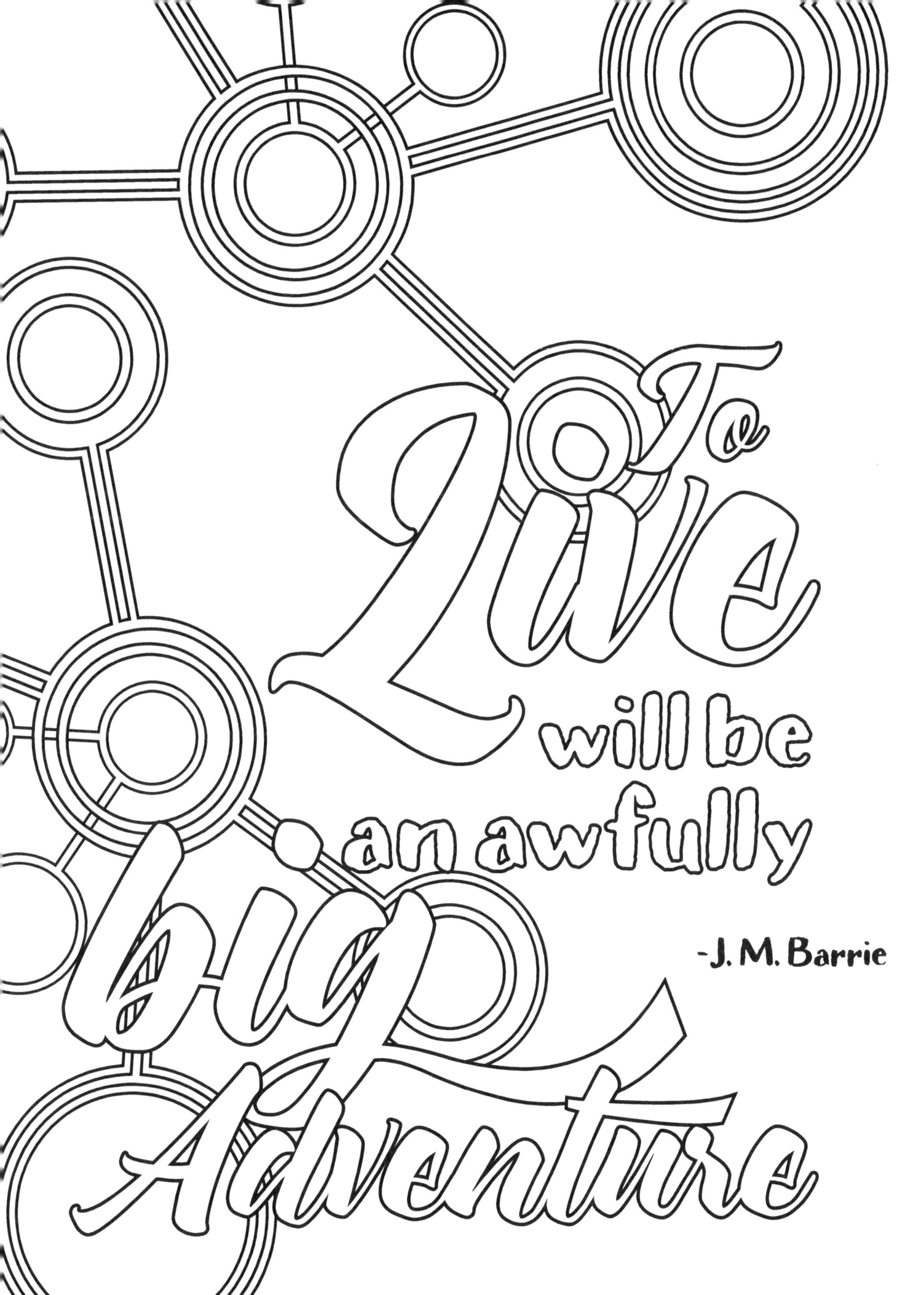

To Live will be an awfully big Adventure

-J. M. Barrie

Describe an adventure, big or small, that changed the way you live your everyday life.

discover

FOR THE CHANGE MAKER

advocate for what you believe in. fight the good fight. empower those around you. be the catalyst for change. inspire the masses. transform mindsets. speak up. stand out. feel your purpose deep inside your bones.

WE ARE THE ONES

we've been waiting for

WE ARE THE CHANGE

that we seek

- BARACK OBAMA

How can you inspire those around you to come together to make the change you want so badly to see?

THE PEOPLE WHO ARE *crazy enough* TO THINK THEY CAN *change the world,* ARE THE ONES WHO DO.

-STEVE JOBS

If you could pick one problem in the world to solve - and consequently change the world - what would it be?

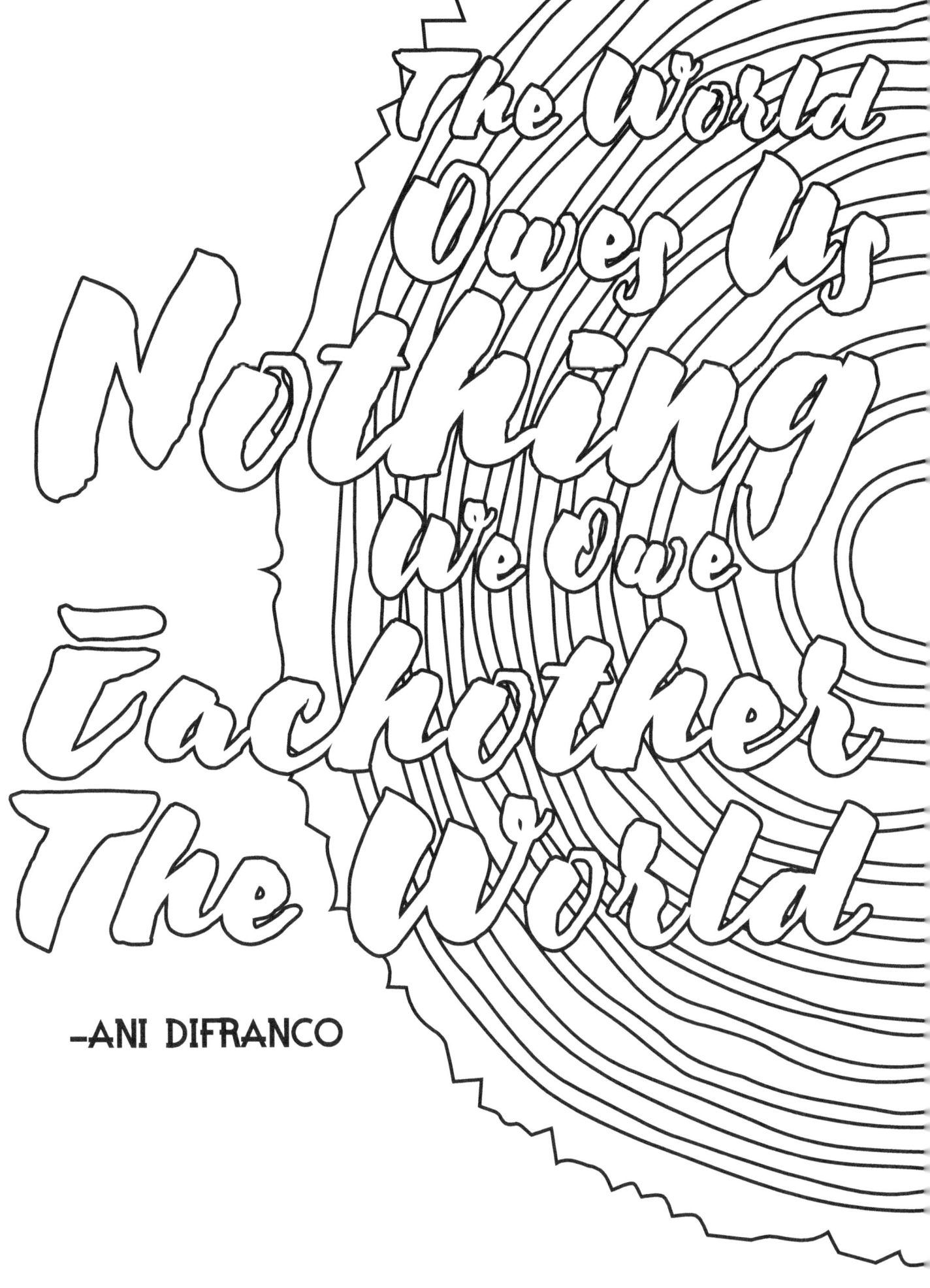

In what ways can you make a contribution to the world around you?

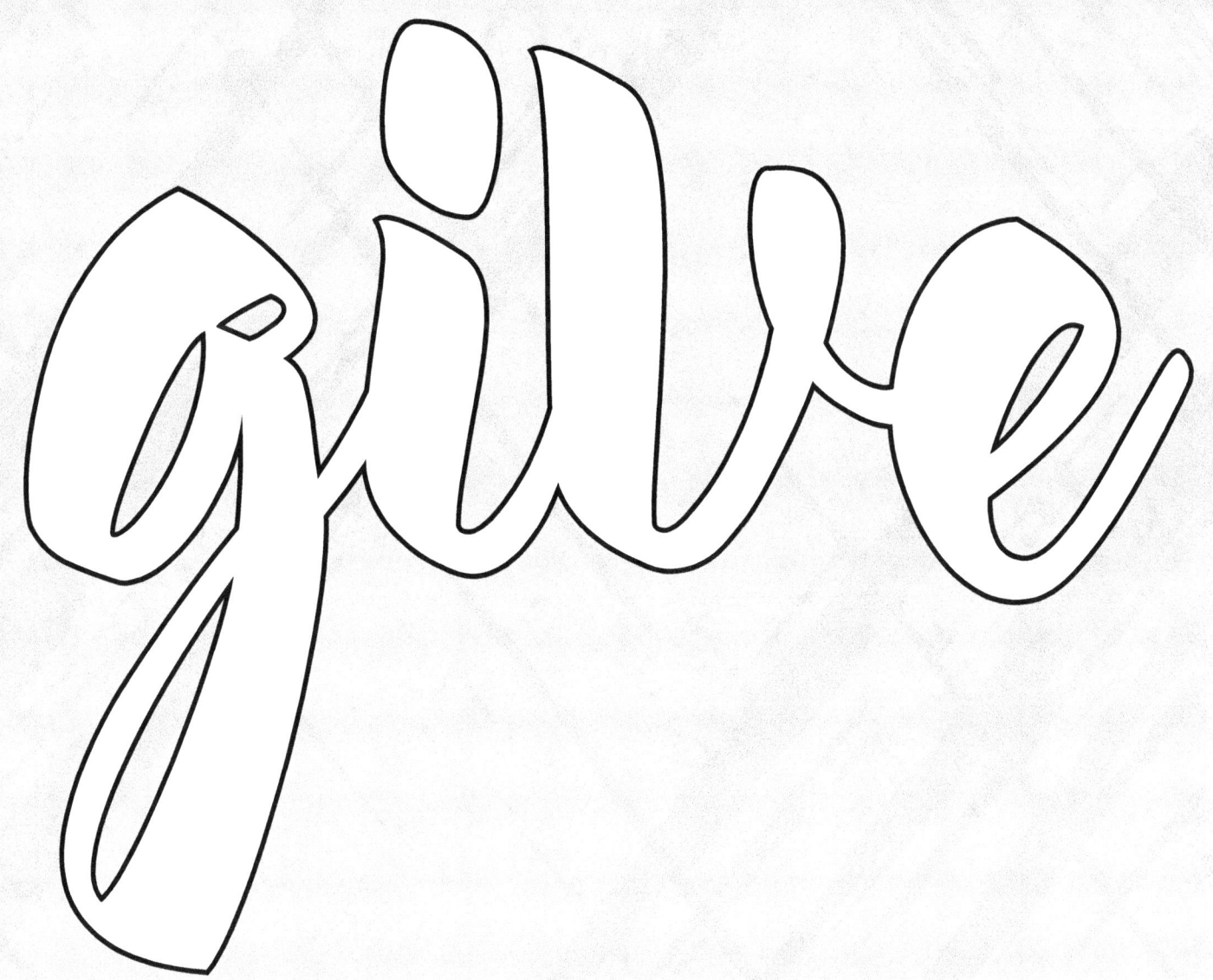

FOR THE REBEL

squash the status quo.
shake the world
by its shoulders.
make noise with
a purpose.
play by your own rules.
question everything.
defy the limits.
forge your own path.
instigate a little madness.

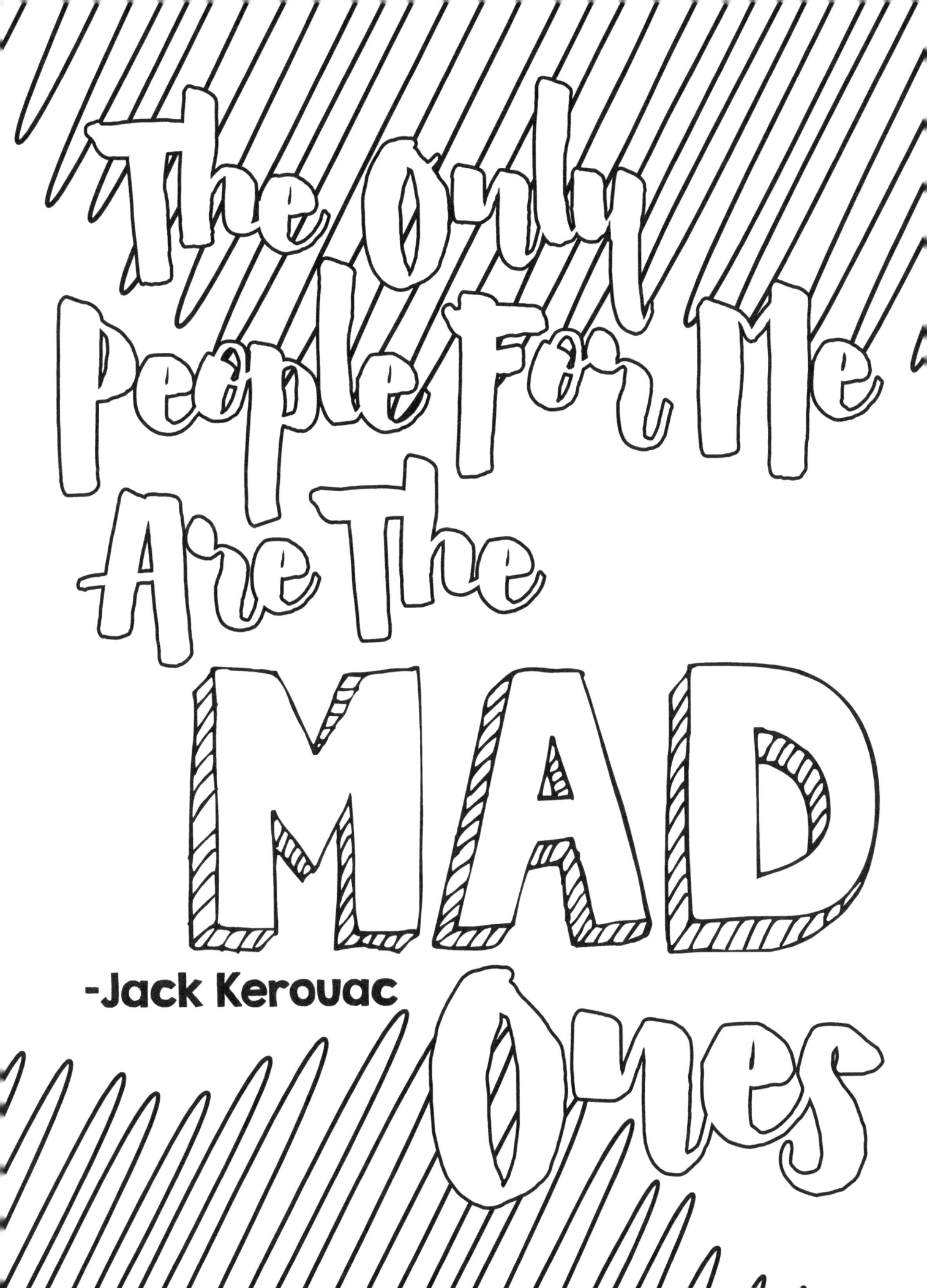

Who are the people in your life that light you up and make you come alive?

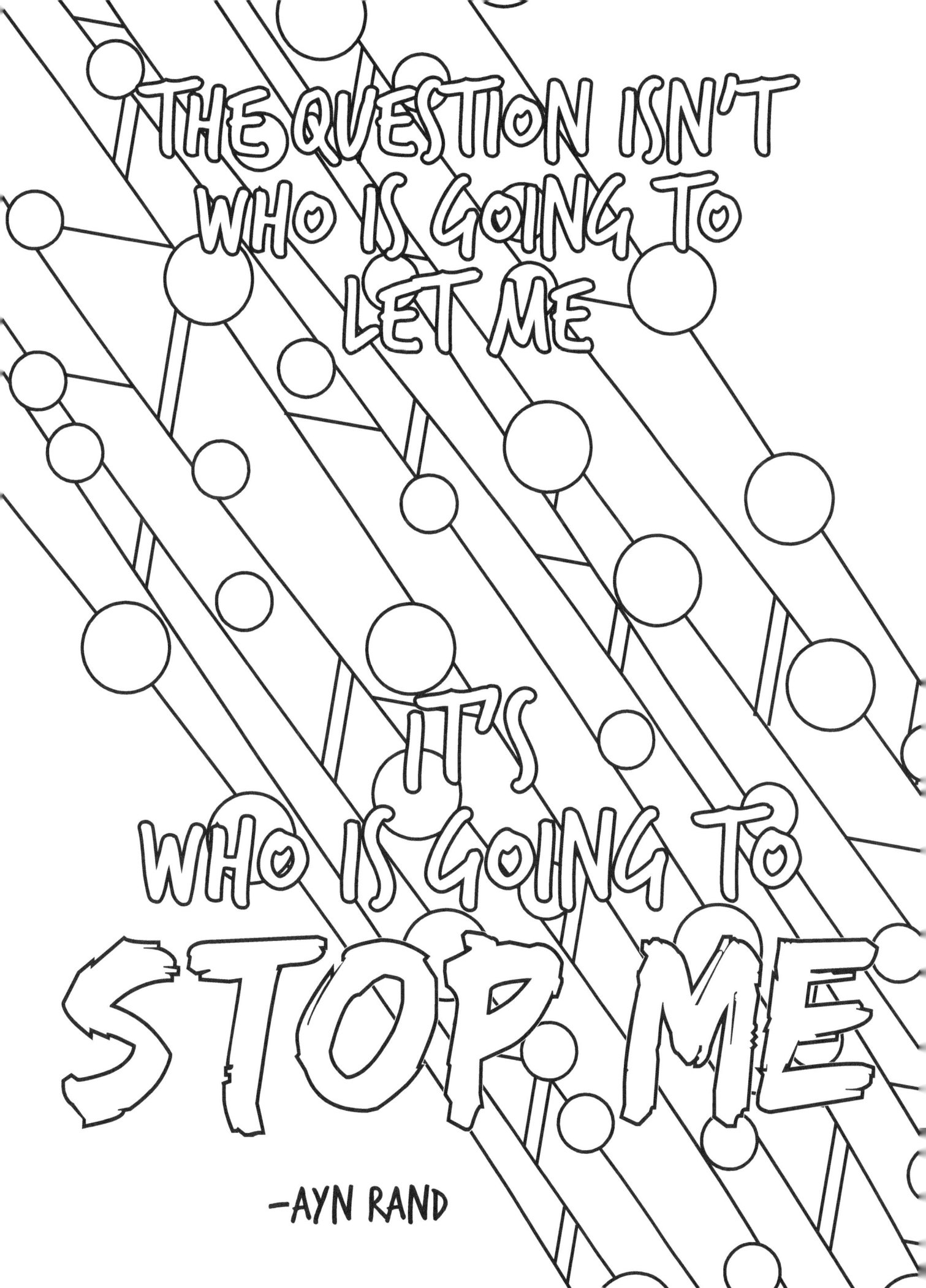

What goals or dreams are you pursuing without a permission slip?

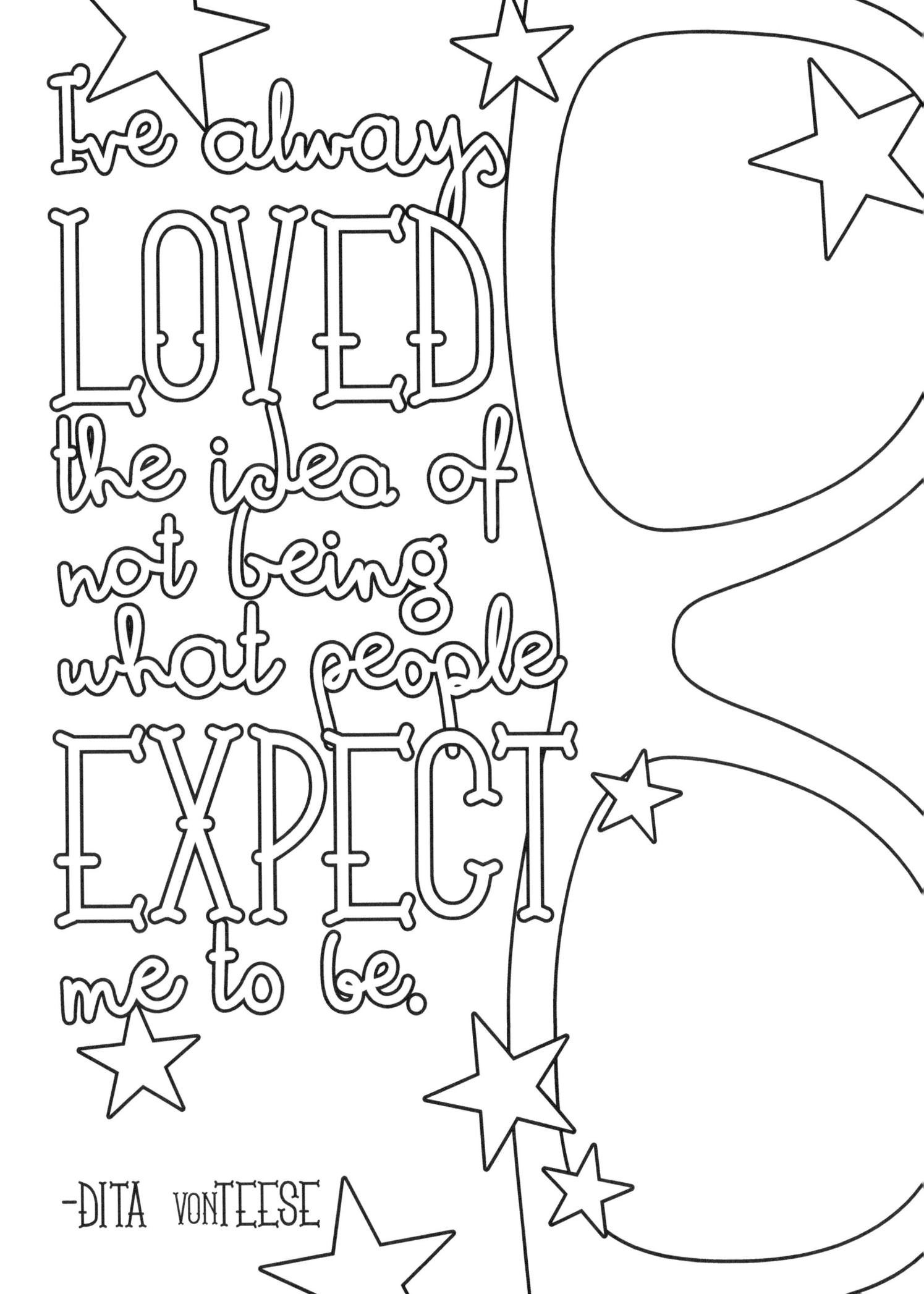

How has being different led you to experience the world in a way others don't/can't?

defy